MW01254806

ANDREW JACKSON

A Life From Beginning to End

Copyright © 2016 by Hourly History

Table of Contents

Introduction

Andrew Jackson may have been the first American president without an impressive pedigree, but he's also the first White House inhabitant to prove that the destiny of the nation would no longer be the exclusive province of the blue-blooded elite. Jackson was no Founding Father, but he was just as fiercely dedicated to the concepts of freedom as any member of that first generation of American patriots. He was a president whose rise to power betokened the courage of his immigrant parents and the dynamic new direction of a nation which was willing, *en masse*, to pull up stakes and venture into the unknown in order to seek a better life for themselves and their families. Jackson was the first president who hailed from neither Massachusetts nor Virginia, but instead from the frontier west of Tennessee. Additionally, when faced with the threat of secession, Jackson declared that the Union must be preserved.

In his lifetime, he was a controversial figure. In modern times, his reputation has come under scrutiny because he was so much a man of his era. He supported states' rights and favored the expansion of slavery in the western territories that would eventually become states. He lived in a century when Native Americans were the enemy, and he treated them accordingly. But it's constricting to view Andrew Jackson in those rigid terms, regardless of how his actions seem to our modern eyes. He changed the course of American history and served as president when the nation was undergoing its raw adolescence. Some of his decisions were astute, others were ruthless, but he was not afraid to act on his convictions. His belief that the common people were the ones who should decide a nation's course came out of his own experience and his own convictions; at a time when the common people were often regarded as the rabble, his view was revolutionary.

Chapter One

The Birth of a Legend

"Remember, remember always, that all of us, and you and I especially, are descended from immigrants and revolutionists."

—Franklin D. Roosevelt

The president who was known as Old Hickory had no choice but to be tough. Born on March 15, 1767, to Scots-Irish immigrants from Ireland, who had arrived with sons Hugh and Robert to settle in the Waxhaws region between the Carolinas, Jackson was the first president whose parents were immigrants. The area where the Jacksons lived was in a remote area that hadn't been surveyed. He may have been born at an uncle's plantation in Lancaster County, South Carolina, or he may have been born in the home of another uncle who lived in North Carolina. Jackson was born just when Tennessee was beginning to be settled as immigrants from Europe, who probably landed in Philadelphia, crossed the Appalachian Mountains to find homes in a region where land was fertile, and there was hope for a better life.

What Tennessee in its frontier days did not offer was an easy life. The people who came to Tennessee did not travel with a wealth of possessions. They possessed little and knew how to manage with what they had. In order to eat, they had to grow their food or hunt it. They had come to conquer the land, but Tennessee did not readily surrender to their efforts as they chopped down the trees and cleared the land for agriculture. The houses were rudimentary, with the family sharing common living space. But they had come not only for prosperity but freedom, and they were willing to work hard in order to raise children who would grow up in liberty.

To the Native American tribes who already occupied the lands, the European settlers were invaders. By settling in Tennessee, the immigrants were violating the English Proclamation of 1763, which denied Americans and immigrants the right to build settlements west of the Appalachian Mountains. As the years passed, Cherokee rights to their own land would diminish. As an adult, Andrew Jackson would play a role in that loss of territory.

It was a generation which knew tragedy. Andrew Jackson was fatherless within three weeks of his birth following the death of the senior Andrew Jackson, who died in an accident when he was 29 years old. Possibly, Andrew Jackson entered the world during the time that his mother was returning home after the burial of his father. But he did not grow up in isolation, as there were numerous Jackson relatives in the area, as it was home to many farmers of Scots-Irish heritage.

The family was poor, and education was not a priority during hard times. His mother had hopes that her young son would become a Presbyterian minister when he was old enough to choose a career, but she must have had to accept the fact that Andrew, with his volatile nature and eagerness to fight, was not destined for the clergy. Andrew was tall, lean, and agile, with red hair and the freckles that go with them, as well as what would become his legendary temper. He was quick, even as a boy, to resort to violence to solve a problem. Throughout his life, he resorted to action rather than thought, with a fearless energy to do what needed to be done.

The American Revolution was in its final years by the time Jackson joined the local militia as a courier at the age of 13. He was captured, along with his brother Robert, by the British when the army headed south and invaded the Carolinas in 1781. Brother Hugh, the eldest of the Jackson sons, had also joined the American cause, perishing at the Battle of Stono Ferry from heatstroke.

The temper that would rule Andrew Jackson throughout his life was just as fierce in his youth: when a British officer ordered the boy to polish the redcoat's boots, Jackson refused. The officer used his sword on Jackson, cutting a gash into his face that sliced the skin all the way to the bone, leaving him with a scar for the rest of his life as a permanent reminder of his reason for hating the British.

While prisoners of the British, both brothers contracted smallpox; during their captivity, the surviving brothers were nearly starved. A prisoner exchange, arranged by their mother, Elizabeth Jackson, released Robert and Andrew from the tender ministrations of the British. The boys had to travel 45 miles to get back home, a journey that they made in pouring rain. Robert died two days after they arrived home; Andrew survived, but his recovery took time. Elizabeth Jackson, believing that Robert would recover, had gone to Charleston to do her part for the American war effort by taking care of the soldiers who had been wounded. But she died of cholera soon after son Robert's death, leaving Jackson an orphan at age 14. The hardships which he and his family endured left him with a virulent antipathy toward the British, an emotion which would come to the fore again when he was an adult fighting the former foe in the War of 1812. For Jackson, the price of American liberty came at great cost.

His uncles took him in when he was left without a mother or brothers. Jackson inherited a small bequest from his grandfather in Ireland, but the money didn't last long. For a time, Jackson made a living as a schoolteacher, although his education had been limited and his affinity for study minimal. Mostly self-taught, as several others in the presidential office would be (most notably Abraham Lincoln), Jackson read the Bible, and as an adult was fond of reading newspapers and the classics. When he was 17, he began the study of law, apprenticing with local lawyers in Salisbury, North Carolina. Three years later, he received a license to practice law in the North Carolina backcountry. Money was tight, and Jackson worked in the general store to supplement his income. As a six-foot-tall redhead, Jackson stood out in a crowd, but his personality always garnered attention. He enjoyed dancing and gambling and was no stranger to good times in local taverns.

Before long, he had attracted the interest of people of influence. John McNairy, who was a friend and a mentor, was elected a Superior Court judge of the North Carolina Western District. The territory extended from the Mississippi River to the Appalachian Mountains. McNairy, needing a representative of the law in the frontier area, chose Jackson. By age 21, Jackson was the prosecuting attorney west of the Appalachian Mountains in North Carolina, in what is now Tennessee. His practice did well enough for him to move to Nashville the next year; the bulk of his practice was debt collection, disputed land claims, and assault charges, but he was very successful at it. He also went into business in 1794, buying and selling the land which wasn't held for the Cherokee and Chickasaw Indians by existing treaties.

It would be the law that would continue to provide a prosperous livelihood for Jackson. In time, he would become a wealthy landowner. In 1803, he purchased the Hermitage, which included 640 acres of land, near Nashville. He would later add 360 acres to the cotton plantation, and slaves to work in the fields and the house. He also began to acquire a network of friends of influence, something that would become the foundation of his involvement in Tennessee politics.

Chapter Two

Jackson the General

"Peace, above all things, is to be desired, but blood must sometimes be spilled to obtain it on equable and lasting terms."

—Andrew Jackson

Politics caught the attention of the young lawyer, and in 1796 he was elected to serve as Tennessee's first U.S. representative. However, he resigned eight months after taking office. Jackson said that he would never again enter public life after he left the House of Representatives, and he returned to the legal profession, where he served as a circuit judge on the Tennessee superior court until 1804. Tennessee was still the frontier at this time, and its citizens had to rise to the occasion when their talents were needed. That occasion came for Andrew Jackson when military service was required, and leaders were called for.

Andrew Jackson was not the man to allow a lack of military experience keep him from the fray. He was brave and decisive, and when facing the enemy, he was committed to overcoming all obstacles until victory was achieved. Tennessee, in the earliest years of the nineteenth century, was a wild, unsettled place, and troops were needed along the frontier. He was appointed a major-general of Tennessee's militia in 1802 when he was thirty-five years old.

In 1812, the United States once again found itself at war with its enemy, Great Britain. For Jackson, this was a time when his own life was in disarray; his political career was in limbo, he had lost standing in society, and he was financially in distress. But the war was about to offer Jackson the opportunity to restore his reputation. Jackson was already perturbed that the national government was unable to protect its people and its property; as the major-general of the Tennessee militia, he would have the opportunity to prove what his country could do, and what he could do to make that happen.

Not everyone was comfortable with Jackson's involvement in the war. There were political events which led President James Madison to wonder if Andrew Jackson's help was worth the potential risk. For one thing, Jackson had continued his friendship with Aaron Burr, the controversial statesman and former Vice President who had killed Alexander Hamilton in a duel a few years before. Even worse, Burr was said to be ambitious to start his own country by trying to persuade the western states to secede from the United States.

But Madison needed help, and by the end of the year 1812, the president commissioned Jackson as a major-general and put him in charge of 1,500 volunteers with orders to head south with the goal of defending the port of New Orleans. But when the War Department decided that there was no genuine threat to New Orleans. Jackson and his forces were dismissed; no provision was made to compensate the soldiers or provide them with the means to obtain food or travel back to Tennessee, even though the route would take them through Indian territory. Jackson vowed that if he had to pay the costs himself, he'd bring his men home. Jackson shared their privations with them, enduring every hardship that they endured, and the men repaid him with the nickname that would stand all his life, Old Hickory, because he was tough as a hickory tree.

Jackson was injured during the war, but his injury came because he could not control his temper or his tongue. When two of the officers in his forces quarreled, Jackson took sides rather than bring the argument to resolution. The disagreement turned to violence in a gunfight on the streets of Nashville, and Jackson ended up with a severe wound in his upper arm.

Tennessee learned that a group of Creek Indians was attacking settlers in Fort Mims, in what is today Alabama. Jackson was ordered to put down the uprising, so in October 1813, he headed south, where he was victorious in battle, defeating the Indians at Tallushatchee and Talladega. Jackson was discovering that he had a flair for leadership and a knack for soldiering. But it was at the Battle of Tallushatchee that the warrior became a father; finding an infant held in the arms of his dead Creek mother, Jackson adopted the child, naming him Lyncoya.

Jackson's foes were not only external ones. The troops were in disagreement over the terms of enlistment. That, and the inability to supply them with their needs meant that Jackson faced desertions among his forces. Twice,

Jackson addressed their threat to return home by threatening to shoot would-be deserters. However, when their terms of enlistment were up, gunfire wouldn't make them stay. Jackson sent an appeal to the Tennessee governor for more troops. The governor came through, and with a force of 5,000, Jackson's volunteers defeated the Creek warriors at Horseshoe Bend, bringing the Creek War to an end in March 1814.

His return to Tennessee was triumphant. He had removed the threat of the Indians attacking, but his victory had accomplished something which would affect the future of Tennessee's economy. With the threat of Indian attack gone, the state could begin to expand its growth through the building of forts and roads.

Although he may not have realized it, his timing was perfect. The War of 1812 against the British, known derisively as "Mr. Madison's War," was going badly. The United States needed a hero, and Andrew Jackson was going to fit the bill very nicely.

With a commission as a major-general in the U.S. Army for the 7th military district, Jackson was in charge of Tennessee, Louisiana and the Mississippi Territory. He was sent to negotiate with the Creek Nation. Under Jackson's negotiations, the Creek chiefs were required to settle in a smaller area that the troops could easily patrol, surrendering 23 million acres of land as part of the arrangement. For the Americans, it was a very good deal. For the Creek tribe, it was a disaster. The Creek would not be the only tribe to lose land because of Andrew Jackson's negotiations.

The British, having ended their war with France, could now focus on the American war, sending troops with the intention of invading. In 1814, the British burned Washington D.C., the nation's capital. Jackson heard that the British were planning to invade the South via Mobile or New Orleans. First, Jackson went to Mobile to strengthen the city's fortifications.

He then, although he was not authorized to do so, invaded Florida, which belonged to Spain. His motive was to get rid of the potential threat from the rumored invasion by the British and also to nullify the dangers of the tribes who were allied with Great Britain and hostile to the Americans. Jackson and his troops headed for Spanish Florida. Jackson captured Pensacola in November 1814 and then set off on the trail of the British, who were on their way to New Orleans.

As he had done in Mobile, Jackson prepared New Orleans for an attack by the British. The Americans, consisting of a military force of regular U.S. troops, Tennessee militia volunteers, with militia from Kentucky, Louisiana and the Mississippi Territory, free blacks, Native Americans, Creoles and even a band of pirates, were outnumbered, not to mention inexperienced, compared to the looming British forces.

The rumors of the invasion were true. The British invasion began on December 14. On December 23, Jackson's forces halted the advance of the British troops, initiating two weeks of battle as the British sought a way through Jackson's defenses to reach New Orleans. On January 8, a full-scale attack by the British was launched.

Jackson's forces were outnumbered two-to-one at the battle. They were not a cohesive fighting unit. Despite these drawbacks, on January 8, 1815, Jackson's 5,000 soldiers defeated the mighty forces of the British at the Battle of New Orleans, forcing the expert soldiers of the British Empire to withdraw from Louisiana. New Orleans was saved. Once again, the Americans had beaten the British.

The peace treaty between the United States and Great Britain had already been signed in Belgium, but slow communication prevented Jackson from knowing that his battle victory was unnecessary. The Treaty of Ghent had brought the war to an end several weeks before Jackson's conclusive victory, although it would not be ratified by Congress until February 16, 1815.

It was not, however, unappreciated. The victory against the traditional foe vaulted Jackson onto the national stage as a hero; not since the glory days of George Washington had the Americans had such a military icon to adore. Congress gave him a gold medal for his achievements. His military prowess also did much to boost the confidence of a very young country which had no longstanding military heritage to boast of, as did its European counterparts. The world saw, through Jackson's boldness, that the Americans could take care of themselves on the field of battle.

Now at peace, the United States military forces were divided into northern and southern divisions; Jackson was given command over the southern division. Jackson perceived a dual threat to the region. One was from

Florida, which was controlled by the Spanish. The other was from the native tribes. His reputation was well known to the tribes, and the Creeks, Cherokees, Chickasaws, and Choctaws signed treaties which left them with significantly reduced land while the United States was able to increase its territory. What would benefit the Americans the most would be the undoing of the tribes, who would eventually be forced to leave their ancestral homes.

Florida was a different matter, and an international one since it belonged to Spain. There was no representative military force in the area, which meant that for the British, there was a way to invade. The Seminole tribe could raid areas in the border regions and then safely return to Spanish Florida.

In 1817, Jackson returned to military leadership during the First Seminole War. Jackson returned to Florida, which was still under the rule of the Spanish, and, acting entirely on his own, he proceeded to capture St. Mark's and Pensacola (for the second time), execute two British subjects because they had provided assistance to the Seminoles, and then overthrew the governor, claiming the land for the United States. Spain was outraged, and President Monroe had a diplomatic crisis on his hands.

Secretary of State John Quincy Adams defended Jackson against the charges of the Spanish; it's likely that Jackson's acts, impulsive though they were, helped the momentum of the American acquisition of land. The Spanish saw the handwriting on the wall, and it was Jackson's hand that revealed the intensity of the desire of the Americans to own Florida. The Adams-Onis Treaty of 1819 gave Florida to the United States, with the United States receiving the favorable acquisition of boundaries.

In June 1821, Jackson resigned his military commission and was named the military governor of Florida, but he accepted the position without enthusiasm. During his stint as the governor, Rachel Jackson, who had gone to Florida to be with him, influenced him to make the sale and consumption of alcohol illegal on Sundays. But when she wanted to return home, Jackson resigned as governor and bought his wife back to the Hermitage.

Chapter Three

Jackson and Politics

*"The planter, the farmer, the mechanic, and the laborer...
form the great body of the people of the United States, they
are the bone and sinew of the countrymen who love liberty
and desire nothing but equal rights and equal laws. "*

—Andrew Jackson

It's unlikely that any of the political seers in 19th century America could have realized that Jackson's actions would directly affect the destiny of the United States. His success in military ventures brought more land to the growing nation, but by securing so much land, a new crop, which would thrive in the southern soil, would eventually bring both prosperity and tragedy to the region: cotton became the dominant agricultural produce in the South. It would, ultimately, expand the number of enslaved peoples, creating an irreparable division between North and South that would only be solved by war.

But those years were in the future. For now, America was bursting with confidence, boosted by the boom in agriculture and manufacturing that strengthened the nation's economic growth. Americans liked the looks of the Tennessee soldier who was known to be forthright, bold, and courageous. Such traits were very attractive to the men who controlled the nation's political process.

Politics in early 19th century America was a rough-and-tumble business. Jackson, who had achieved a national image thanks to his military prowess, was a nominee for the office of president in 1824 and won the popular vote. However, as no candidates won a majority of votes in the Electoral College, the election went to the House of Representatives to decide. John Quincy Adams was named the victor, thanks to support from Henry Clay, Speaker of the House. Adams then named Clay to the office of Secretary of State, which outraged Jackson's supporters; they labeled the deal as the Corrupt Bargain in the press. Jackson himself resigned from the Senate as a result of the machinations.

But there would be another election, and the Democrats knew who their candidate would be. In a time when politics was not regarded for its refined practices, the election of 1828 is viewed as one of the nastiest in American history. The opponents, the aloof and irascible John Quincy Adams of the Adams political dynasty, and Andrew Jackson, a hard-edged westerner with a reputation for violence, were destined to meet again in competition after the deal-making that had given John Quincy Adams the office when the Electoral College could not award a majority of votes to a winning candidate.

The political issues which drove the campaign did not strongly divide the candidates. They both believed in keeping protective tariffs, and both supported the building of America. But personality outweighed the issues. Jackson was the candidate who had attracted the attention of Americans, and the Adams faction, recognizing this, made sure that the public was informed of the past scandal surrounding Jackson's wife.

Jackson's enemies and opponents resurrected the label of bigamist against Rachel Jackson because she and Jackson had married before she was legally divorced from her abusive first husband. A newspaper editorial asked, "Ought a convicted adulteress and her paramour husband to be placed in the highest offices of this free and Christian land?"

To combat the calumny, Jackson fought back with an early version of what would now be a public relations campaign. His supporters gave speeches that criticized the tactics of men who showed a lack of chivalry in criticizing the gentle Mrs. Jackson. These were years when women lived sheltered lives away from public view; to be accused as an adulteress was a shocking turn of events for a woman who preferred to live privately. Of the accusations, Rachel said that her husband's enemies had dipped their pens in wormwood.

The Jackson campaign made the novel attempt to enlist female support for Rachel by encouraging the wives of Jackson backers to come to Washington DC to attend the inauguration and show their support for Mrs. Jackson. It would be up to the voters to decide whether the reputation of Jackson's wife would decide the election.

Jackson had all the qualities for president that a vigorous young nation was looking for in a leader. Not only was he a military hero, but he had served in both the

American Revolution and the War of 1812, and if elected, he would be the only president who had done so. He espoused the rights of the common man and had much in common with them. The people who supported Jackson called themselves Democrats. When his political foes called him a jackass, the candidate promptly claimed the animal as the symbol of the party, a tradition which continues into modern politics. Jackson and his running mate John C. Calhoun of South Carolina won in a landslide, making Jackson the first president elected from the American frontier.

The inauguration was as historic as Jackson's victory. The first president elected to office who did not hail from the Eastern coast, who had no longstanding tradition or heritage, attracted the loyalty of Americans who were not content to sit on the sidelines as their hero achieved his victory. Margaret Smith, a woman who was an eyewitness to much of American's history, wrote to a friend, describing the inauguration: "Ladies fainted, men were seen with bloody noses, and such a scene of confusion took place as is impossible to describe."

The inauguration began decorously enough. Thousands were gathered at the Capitol waiting for Jackson to appear. He entered, surrounded by the Supreme Court justices, and bowed to the assembly, which responded with shouts of acclamation. He took the oath of office in a low voice that could only be heard by those who were near him; he kissed the Bible, and once again, bowed to the people who were watching. After he gave his inaugural speech, the barrier that separated him from the audience was broken down, and the crowd rushed up the Capitol steps to shake his hand, trapping Jackson in their midst. Finally, he made his way through the crowd and mounted his horse to leave. Following behind him were children, men, and women both black and white, farmers and gentry, people on foot and people in carriages and on horseback, all heading to the White House.

The crowd was so huge that Smith was not able to go into the White House. Three hours later, her efforts were more successful. "But what a scene did we witness! The Majesty of the People had disappeared, and a rabble, a mob, of boys, Negroes, women, children, scrambling, fighting, romping. What a pity, what a pity! No arrangements had been made, no police officers placed on duty, and the whole house had been inundated by the rabble mob." Several thousand dollars in damages, in the form of broken china and glass, were the result as the celebrants, eager to receive their cake, ice cream, and lemonade, struggled together for their share. Smith wrote that "those who got in could not get out by the door again but had to scramble out of windows."

Jackson himself was pressed against the wall by the mob and was only able to escape when a group of men formed a wall around him, creating a barrier to protect him. Jackson managed to get out by leaving through another door, where he then retreated to his lodgings, not spending his first night as president in the White House. Smith's summary was astute: "Ladies and gentleman, only had been expected at this Levee, not the people en masse.

But it was the People's day, and the People's President, and the People would rule."

No elitist himself, Jackson wanted to share his victory with the public. However, this was a time of hard drinking and rough ways. This time, the nickname that was bestowed upon Jackson was less flattering: he was called "King Mob" because of the rambunctious behavior of his celebrating supporters. This mob had elected him president; it remained to be seen how he would govern his constituents. But he would do so as a man in mourning, without his wife at his side. He blamed his enemies and their insults for the death of his wife, who had passed away before she could join him as First Lady.

Chapter Four

Jackson's Home Life

"A being so gentle and so virtuous slander might wound,
but could not dishonor."

—Epitaph on Rachel Jackson's tombstone

When he was a young man on the frontier, Jackson fell in love with a married woman, Rachel Donelson Robards. Neither one of them, however, realized that she was still married to her first husband.

Rachel had been born in Virginia in 1767, but when she was 12, she and her family moved to live in the wilderness of Tennessee. Along with 600 people, the travelers journeyed on 40 flatboats and canoes along the Holston River to the Cumberland River to settle in Fort Nashborough, which would later be renamed Nashville. The Donelsons were a family of prominence in the new town of Nashville, and would be leaders in business, politics and civic organizations.

Her father, Colonel John Donelson, was a hunter, surveyor, and a member of the Virginia Assembly, as well as a co-founder of the city of Nashville. Education on the frontier was difficult to come by, and as the fourth of twelve children, Rachel would have been busy helping with the household. She learned to read and, like many women on the frontier, the Bible was her main choice of reading material. Frontier life was demanding and violent; in 1786, her father was murdered on his way back home to Tennessee from Virginia, and his killers were never discovered.

When Rachel was 17 years old, she married a man named Lewis Robards, the son of a prominent family. However, he was an unreasonably jealous man; within two years, they had separated. Rachel's family said that he was physically abusive to his wife and that Rachel had fled back to her mother's home for her own safety. Because she feared for her life, she was relieved to hear that he was filing a petition to divorce her.

When Jackson moved to Nashville to practice law, he lodged in the boarding house that Rachel's mother operated. In 1791, Jackson married Rachel, but two years later, they discovered that while it was true that Robards had obtained permission to file for divorce, the decree had only been placed on the docket but had not proceeded any further. Robards brought suit against his wife, charging her with adultery. Upon his return to Nashville, he claimed that she was inappropriately intimate with Jackson. After the divorce had become official, the Jacksons were legally married in 1794. Their premature first marriage was a mistake that was easily made in a time when travel and communication were both arduous and primitive on the frontier, but it was a costly one for a man with political aspirations and a quick temper.

Jackson was quick to defend his wife against accusers. Years before, Jackson confronted one of Rachel's detractors, killing Charles Dickinson in a duel that left the future president with a bullet in his chest for the remainder of his life. The quarrel had originally begun in an argument over a horse race, but as soon as Dickinson turned the topic to Rachel's past, Jackson demanded satisfaction. Dickinson was a marksman of note, while Jackson was not. But Jackson elected to take the first shot anyway because he believed that he was determined enough to endure whatever happened, and then he would have the opportunity to kill the man who insulted Rachel.

Dickinson's first shot hit Jackson in the chest. Jackson fired next, with a shot that killed the man who insulted his beloved wife. Although a man of impulse, Jackson was canny. He had dressed his slender, 145-pound frame in dark blue trousers and frock coat; Dickenson, gauging the position of Jackson's heart from his garment, miscalculated because of the loose fit of the coat. Still, Jackson was gravely wounded; his boot was filled with blood, and two of his ribs were shattered. For the rest of his life, he would suffer discomfort from the wounds he suffered and the bullet that remained within him, but he had had satisfaction. Duels were an accepted means of dealing with insults, but they still aroused scandal, and after the Dickinson duel, Jackson went home to the Hermitage where he would be out of the public eye.

Rachel Jackson herself was said to be a kind and hospitable woman, welcoming guests to the Hermitage, the estate Jackson had purchased in 1804. Rachel had a large family, and her relatives were frequent visitors. Rachel stayed at home while her husband was busy with his military and political careers, but managing the

Hermitage, with its household tasks, farming, and overseeing the slaves, would have been her work. She missed her husband during his absences and chided him for answering the call of duty. "Do not, my beloved husband, let the love of country, fame, and honor make you forget that you have me. Without you I would think them all empty shadows. You will say this is not the language of a patriot, but it is the language of a faithful wife, one I know you esteem and love." Rachel was said to be able to gentle her husband's fiery impulses with a gesture or a word, preventing him from becoming embroiled in even more dramatic encounters with people who opposed him.

But Rachel herself had a political background; her relatives were involved in Nashville politics, and according to tradition, she had been a guest with her family at the homes of Virginia's celebrated statesmen George Washington and Patrice Henry, who were her father's colleagues in the Virginia House of Burgesses.

Childless, the Jacksons adopted an Indian orphan he found during the Creek war and, in 1809 they had adopted the son of Rachel's brother, who was named Andrew Jackson, Jr.

The vicious campaign took its toll on Rachel, who was forced to endure the calumny of Jackson's political enemies. Her health had been poor for several years, and she had a fatal heart attack in December 1828. She was buried on Christmas Eve, two months before she would have gone to Washington D. C. to be First Lady. For her burial, she was attired in the white dress she had bought to wear for Jackson's inauguration as president. Jackson buried her in her garden at the Hermitage. He blamed those who had slandered her for her death, saying, "May God Almighty forgive her murderers as I know she forgave them. I never can." But Rachel's ill health also had physical causes; she smoked a corncob pipe, and her smoking likely contributed to her failing health.

The mayor and aldermen of Nashville passed a resolution that encouraged the citizens to abstain from their daily business on the day of her funeral, and to toll the church bells during the hour of her burial.

Ten thousand people, black and white, attended her funeral. The governor of Tennessee, Sam Houston, was one of her pallbearers. At her ceremony, Jackson said, "I am now President of the United States … and if it had been God's will, I would have been grateful for the privilege of taking her to my post of honor and seating her by my side … For myself, I bow to God's will and go alone to the place of new and arduous duties."

He never remarried. He carried a miniature of Rachel's likeness every day; at night, it was placed on the table by his bedside. When his presidency ended, and he returned home, Jackson visited her grave every evening as long as his health allowed him to do so.

Chapter Five

Jackson's First Term

"It was settled by the Constitution, the laws, and the whole practice of the government that the entire executive power is vested in the President of the United States."

—Andrew Jackson

Jackson became president as the leader of his party and the master of his administration. His enemies would deride him as King Andrew I for his firm, perhaps authoritarian, grip on power; he used his presidential veto power without a qualm, and he regarded Congress as his subordinate. Jackson did not intend to serve the nation as a mere administrator of policy; he intended to define it. But not all of a president's decisions are based on politics.

Jackson was hot-headed and strong-willed and proved an inexorable opponent to his enemies. He was also chivalrous. Those traits collided early in his presidency in what became known as the "Petticoat War," an episode which rocked Washington D.C. and split the president's cabinet. It concerned a woman named Margaret "Peggy" Eaton, who, unlike the wellborn ladies with political husbands, had less grand origins as the daughter of a tavern keeper. Although she was married to a 39-year old Navy purser, seventeen-year-old Peggy continued to work at her father's tavern while her husband was out to sea. In

1818, the couple met the widowed senator, John Eaton. Eaton and Peggy began spending time together while her husband was at sea, and rumors began to fly that Peggy and the senator were more than just friends.

When Peggy's husband died under mysterious conditions in 1828, Peggy, instead of spending a year in mourning as was the custom, married Senator Eaton. The reaction from the political wives was swift and damning, and the senator's new wife was shunned in social circles. Jackson saw the attacks on Peggy Eaton in the same light as the attacks against his beloved wife, Rachel, and his chivalrous instincts were aroused.

Jackson, a friend of the Eatons, named the senator to the post of Secretary of War. The Washington D.C. ladies had already snubbed Peggy by refusing to attend her wedding, and Eaton's appointment to the presidential Cabinet ratcheted the snubbing another level up the social ladder. Mrs. Eaton had offended propriety, and she would be punished for her transgressions.

For two years, the "Petticoat War" continued as the ladies who snubbed Peggy Eaton and the ones who supported her mirrored their husbands' positions in the president's favor. The Vice President's wife was one of Peggy Eaton's most vehement critics, and her refusal to acknowledge the Secretary of War's wife social cost Vice President John Calhoun his office as he fell out of favor with Jackson. The fall from grace likely affected Calhoun's future presidential aspirations as well. Jackson's political friend Martin Van Buren, a widower who supported Mrs.

Eaton, was Jackson's vice presidential running mate in the 1832 election.

The Eaton affair ended when Jackson's entire cabinet resigned, some by choice, others because they had no choice. Jackson had cast his lot with the Eatons, and he expected his administration to do likewise or suffer the consequences. Eaton and Van Buren got the resignations rolling so that the president would be able to request that all the members of the Cabinet resign, bringing the Eaton scandal to an end and allowing Jackson to reorganize his government.

The "Petticoat War" was not the only tempestuous issue of Jackson's first term. Jackson intended to democratize federal office-holding by removing lifetime recipients of government offices and replacing them with what he called qualified applicants. Patronage was commonplace in politics, but Jackson's reforms looked more like rewards for supporters who had benefitted him during his campaign rather than an attempt to clean up corruption. When the process was criticized, one of Jackson's supporters replied that "To the victor belongs the spoils of the enemy." Jackson didn't believe that his supporters had less than altruistic motives for wanting political offices. During his second term, an appointee who was named the collector of the New York City customhouse made off with over one million dollars, an amount which, at that time, was wealth on a massive scale.

Jackson was unable to realize that appointing people to offices based solely on the recommendations of his supporters inevitably meant that patronage had merely acquired a new format. But he had other goals to achieve as president which were guaranteed to stir up a reaction from his political adversaries.

One of the first issues to address was that of protective tariffs. The country supported its economic growth by issuing transportation subsidies and protective tariffs, which benefitted American manufacturers. Since manufacturing was stronger in the North, these policies were resented by the South, which felt that northern growth was achieved at the expense of the South. Beginning with the Maysville Road Bill in 1830, Jackson did veto road and canal bills. He was himself a supporter of lower tariffs, but a crisis was looming which would force Jackson to support the nation, rather than his southern homeland when South Carolina blocked the collection of tariffs within the state.

Jackson's vice president, John C. Calhoun, supported his home state when South Carolina passed a measure which nullified the tariffs, going so far as to threaten to secede from the Union. Jackson was a southerner, and he agreed that the tariff was too high. But secession was not acceptable; Jackson threatened to enforce federal law in Calhoun's state. Jackson proclaimed that the Union could not be divided and that nullification of the existing tariff was treason.

The tension between the president and his vice president was also apparent. In 1830, when the two were at a celebration of the birthday of Thomas Jefferson, the event was an occasion for speeches, including those on states' rights and nullification. Jackson responded with a toast. "Our union, it must be preserved." His vice president responded with a toast of his own: "The union, next to our liberty, most dear."

Calhoun resigned as vice president on December 28, 1832; he had already been replaced on the ticket, and the office of vice president would be held by New York's Martin Van Buren. But Calhoun's influence in government was not over, as he had been named to serve as a senator from Georgia.

In 1830, Congress passed the Indian Removal Act, which granted the president the authority to claim ownership of all Indian lands east of the Mississippi River and giving the tribes new land west of the Mississippi River. In 1832, the last year of Jackson's first term as president, the Supreme Court ruled in *Worcester v. Georgia* that the state's law requiring white residents who wished to reside on Cherokee land to obtain a license to do so was a violation of Cherokee rights. According to the Supreme Court, the Cherokee tribe was its own nation. It was subject to the federal government's authority, but not to state governments.

Some of the political concerns which rose in the first term would be resolved in Jackson's second, and it was soon obvious that he would have that second term. Jackson defeated his opponent Henry Clay in 1832, gaining 56 percent of the popular vote, along with almost five times as many Electoral College votes.

Chapter Six

Jackson's Second Term

"I have always been afraid of banks."

—Andrew Jackson

The second term of President Jackson continued as if there had been no interruption. Henry Clay's bill to lower tariffs passed in February 1833. The passage of the Force Bill just over a week later authorized the president to use force, if required, for the implementation of tariffs in South Carolina. The compromise of a small reduction in the tariff, balanced by a provision granting the President the authority to use force if needed when federal laws were flouted, averted the crisis, but it was a harbinger of things to come as the battle between federal authority and states' rights, the cornerstone of the Civil War, would continue to be waged between the regions. But Jackson's resolve had carried the day; the frontier president was given credit for preserving the Union.

Jackson was much more tolerant toward the issue of state's rights when the state of Georgia claimed millions of acres of land that, according to federal law, belonged to the Cherokee tribe. The Supreme Court ruled that Georgia had no authority over the tribal lands, but Jackson refused to enforce the ruling. The Cherokees had already recognized that, to survive, they would have to come to terms with the presence of the white man on the lands that the tribes had called home.

They began to try to assimilate. Moravian missionaries taught the Indians how Europeans lived and farmed and worshiped. The Cherokee, along with the Creeks, Chickasaws, Seminoles, and Choctaw, became known as the Five Civilized Tribes for their efforts. The Cherokees adopted a constitutional government and developed a written language, further adopting the ways of the white man. But for Americans, and particular for Georgians, this was futile. All they knew or cared to know was that Indians were savages. More to the point, these savages owned land that Americans coveted. One of the foundations of Jackson's presidency was the goal of removing all Indians in the Southeast, a goal which was part of the motivation for the 1830 Indian Removal Act.

The Cherokees did not meekly submit. Using the political knowledge they'd gained by studying the white man's ways, they sent their chief, John Ross, a mixed-blood Cherokee who spoke English and learned the law, to Washington D.C. to plead their cause. But when the Congress failed to be receptive, they took their case to the Supreme Court. Chief Justice John Marshall agreed with Ross' arguments, and the Court ruled that the federal government, not the states, held jurisdiction over the Cherokee nation. Jackson paid no attention and supported Georgia in its activities against the Cherokee.

Another Cherokee leader by the name of Major Ridge went to Washington because he believed that the tribe was better off selling their land; the Americans were simply too powerful to fight, and there were too many of them, with more arriving daily. He approached Congress and negotiated a treaty, selling the land for $5 million. The Cherokee National Council rejected the treaty, but it was too late. Congress ratified it, and Jackson's goal was in motion. The Cherokees had three years to move west.

Jackson wanted the Indian lands, but he had other goals which he pursued passionately as well. The battle lines between the Democrats of Andrew Jackson and the Whigs led by Henry Clay and Daniel Webster were vividly demarcated on the issue of the Bank of the United States. For Jackson, the bank was a symbol of the power and privilege of the elite, the enemy of the common man. Jackson believed that the bank advanced a few at the expense of the many.

Jackson was firmly opposed to the existence of a national bank. The Second Bank of the United States, a corporation which was chartered by Congress, provided the nation with its paper currency and managed the finances of the federal government. In 1832 Jackson, echoing the sentiments of Thomas Jefferson - who believed that a national bank was unconstitutional - vetoed the bill that would have extended the Bank's charter beyond its 1836 expiration date. The following year, he transferred the deposits of the federal government to banks which were chartered by the states. The move caused a financial panic, which led to a depression and caused the Senate to censure the president in 1834.

Jackson was opposed to paper currency. He demanded that the country return to hard money, or gold and silver. In 1836 he issued a Specie Circular, which required that the sale of western public lands had to be paid in coin.

A man who blazed new trails in politics, Jackson is remembered for the many firsts which he brought to the presidency. He was also the first president who faced an attempted assassination, although, as only Andrew Jackson could, he dealt with the would-be assassin with characteristic resilience. Jackson was on his way back from the funeral of a member of Congress. A man named Richard Lawrence shot at him, but the gun misfired. Jackson, then 67 years old, used his cane to defend himself against his attacker. Lawrence was able to fire at Jackson again, but once again the gun misfired.

By that time, the President's aides had managed to grab hold of the assailant, but the damage was done. Not physical damage, as Jackson was unharmed, but damage of another sort. Jackson was convinced that Lawrence, who in all probability was simply a man of mental instability, had been procured by Jackson's political enemies to assassinate him; this was at the time of the Bank crisis, and the Whigs and Democrats were fiercely opposed to one another's stances. Lawrence spent the rest of his life in a mental institution, but the hostile political environment led Vice President Van Buren to carry loaded pistols with him whenever he went to the Senate.

Perhaps Jackson's relationships with his adversaries would have been different had Rachel survived to serve as First Lady. As a widower, although he had lost his wife,

Jackson called upon Rachel's niece, Emily Donelson, to act as hostess for White House social events. She was a poised young woman, 21 years old, who brought her husband and four children (three were born in the White House) with her. The president was her Uncle Andrew, and she was not afraid to speak her mind, even when her views differed from those of the President. But some accounts say that her hostile treatment of Peggy Eaton in the "Petticoat War" cost her the position of White House hostess. Other accounts, however, say that failing health meant that she could no longer serve as hostess. In 1836, she died of tuberculosis.

The closing months of Jackson's presidency saw his daughter-in-law, Sarah Yorke Jackson, perform the social duties that had previously fallen to Emily before her death. Jackson's son had married Sarah Yorke in 1831; the President was not able to attend the ceremony, but he sent a friend to attend the wedding, presenting the bride with a pearl ring which had a locket containing a lock of the President's hair. After the wedding, the newlyweds headed to the White House; Jackson embraced his new daughter-in-law, greeting her from the front steps. He held parties in her honor before the couple returned to the Hermitage to manage the estate while the President was in Washington D.C.; when their first child was born in 1832, they named her Rachel.

Chapter Seven

Jackson Returns to Tennessee

"Heaven will be no heaven to me if I do not meet my wife there."

—Andrew Jackson

Just as Jackson seemed to exemplify the vigor and energy of the new country, he was also an innovator to the office of the presidency. He was the first president to ride a train and the second to be photographed. The White House that he left, with indoor toilets and running water that had been added during his tenure, was a more modern building than it had been when he moved in. He had done much to transform the office he had occupied, both politically and aesthetically.

Jackson's successor, Martin Van Buren, won the 1836 election for president, just as Jackson had intended, and Andrew Jackson went home, leaving Washington D.C. still tremendously popular. Before he left, he delivered his Farewell Address in 1837, which recalled his views on the danger of the banks, as he warned of the threat of what he called the "money power." Jackson's distrust of the financial institutions of the country set him on the offensive as he accused banks, chartered corporations, and turnpike and canal companies of being oppressive institutions which were a threat to liberty. Jackson's hostility toward the national bank and his removal of the bank's deposits set off an economic crisis which lasted past his presidency. The state banks into which the federal money had been deposited were flush with funds, and their reckless spending led to a land speculation boom in the west. The Panic of 1837, just as Van Buren was taking over, would leave financial uncertainty into the next decade.

Although he was no longer in office, Jackson's actions as the president continued to affect the nation. In 1838, General Winfield Scott and 7,000 federal troops were sent to force the Cherokees to move to the Indian territory west of the Mississippi. Approximately 18,000 Cherokee were gathered into forts en route to their new destination. So many died on the first march of 800 miles that Chief John Ross begged the general to let him organize his people into smaller groups who would be able to find food as they traveled. Scott, who was not in favor of this mission anyway but had to obey the orders he had been given, agreed with the suggestion posed by John Ross.

Although he was no longer president, Jackson retained a political interest in the decisions of his successor. Van Buren had been loyal to Jackson and was the recipient of Jackson's advice, but it was to no avail when Van Buren was defeated for re-election in 1840. However, when the winning candidate, William Henry Harrison, who like Jackson was a military hero, died suddenly after becoming president, and John Tyler became president, Jackson's advice was again sought.

As long as he lived, Jackson was a symbol to other Americans. He appeared at the 25th anniversary of the Battle of New Orleans to receive the plaudits of his country. He was also occupied, during his remaining years, in arranging his political papers and working with an author for a biography of his life.

His health was never good, but his determination was indomitable. The bullet from his duel with Dickenson was never removed, but it was not the only bullet in his body. In 1813, he had been shot in a gunfight in Nashville. Jackson had refused to allow the doctors to amputate, and in just over a month, he was back in command of his troops. However, by 1831, the bullet was moving; it needed to come out. The doctor was summoned to the White House, as Jackson refused to go to Philadelphia for the removal because of his concern about how it would be interpreted politically. There was no anesthesia to numb the pain; Jackson bared his arm, the surgeon made the incision and squeezed, and the bullet came out, providing the president with relief. The other bullet would remain lodged inside him.

Jackson's physical health was much more compromised than anyone would have supposed. He endured chronic abdominal pain and diarrhea. He had suffered smallpox as a youth and contracted malaria and dysentery during his Florida military campaigns. He was a smoker and refused to give up the habit, even though tobacco gave him headaches. He also refused to give up his coffee. In 1845, he began to suffer from shortness of breath. Several months before his death, his feet and legs swelled, followed by edema in his hands and abdomen, leaving him unable to lie flat. At night, he had to be propped up with pillows.

Jackson was a realist, and he was prepared for death. In 1831, he had hired an architect to build a tomb for him and Rachel. The Greek design that the architect followed may have been based on the wallpaper that Rachel had chosen for the entrance hall of the Hermitage. As the work progressed, Jackson's letters home from Washington D.C. had asked for updates on the building, which finished in the summer of 1832. After the tomb had been built, the landscaping began. He restored the garden that had been a favorite place for Rachel, with hickory trees and willows planted near the tomb. In a letter to Andrew, Jr., Jackson wrote: "How I am delighted to hear that the garden has regained its former appearance that it always possessed whilst your dear mother was living." When his health permitted, he made daily visits to the tomb. As his health declined, he was able to view the tomb from his office.

Jackson died in 1845, his death attributed to lead poisoning from the bullet that had been lodged in his body since his duel with Charles Dickenson. His pet parrot, Poll, had to be taken from the funeral service because he began to swear at the people who were assembled to mourn the death of a president. He was buried at Rachel's side in the garden tomb at the Hermitage.

Andrew Jackson had fathered no children himself, but he regarded his adopted children as his own. Jackson had intended to send Lyncoya, the Creek infant that he had adopted, to West Point, but was not able to follow through on his intentions. The boy died of tuberculosis in 1828.

Andrew Jackson, Jr., the son of Rachel's brother who had been adopted by the Jacksons, inherited the Hermitage after his father's death.

Conclusion

Jackson's Legacy

"I thank God that my life has been spent in a land of liberty and that He has given me a heart to love my country with the affection of a son."

—Andrew Jackson

The office of President of the United States was a very different entity after the Jackson years than it had been under the preceding occupants of the office. Jackson saw power entirely regarding what he believed was right, and he made his executive decisions accordingly. He was an energetic, rather than a theoretical, leader. The controversy which had engulfed him throughout his life was just as virulent during his terms in office, but he was no imposter to leadership. A president didn't just enforce the laws: he made them.

Jackson believed in the common man, not the elite. His presidency supported democracy as he believed it was meant to be practiced, not as the province of the rich and powerful, but as the birthright of ordinary people. It was the people, Jackson held, who had the power to shape the nation.

Historians may doubt the morality of his effect, but no one can contest the concrete results of his presidency. He paid off the national debt, expanded the boundaries of the nation, issued a new currency, and made America's ties with foreign nations stronger. He was also, in an abstract way, one of the architects of the American myth. If a man proved himself willing to work hard, he could not only succeed in this new country, but he could rise to a position of power. In the nations of the Old World, where inherited land and titles dictated the path to empowerment, there was no fresh blood infusing upward mobility. Americans believed, because they had witnessed the process in men like Jackson, that a man could be born with nothing, but could profit himself by applying himself to the endless task of building his country. That alluring motif would inspire the men of the United States (and the women as well, disenfranchised though they were from even the humblest rungs of the power ladder), but also the peoples of other nations. Immigrants would look to America to rebuild lives that were doomed to poverty and despair in their own homelands, and the nineteenth and twentieth centuries would continue to see a flow of settlers who left home to find a better life.

Jackson was not, however, a visionary: slavery continued to be an economic factor, rather than a moral quagmire, for Jackson's era. Native Americans lost more and more territory and sovereignty as the young country expanded at the expense of the natives who had been there first. The movements that would soon blossom in support of the abolition of slavery and the rights of women were on the horizon, but under Jackson, society was dominated by white men who wielded the power.

Jackson saw nothing wrong in awarding government offices to his supporters, and replaced many of these officials with his own people, beginning what would become known as the spoils system. He was, in this instance, true to his Southern beliefs, as he supported the rights of the states over the federal and judicial authorities. He used his veto power without a qualm, vetoing more bills than had all of the previous presidents combined. He opposed legislation which threatened slavery, supported the availability of cheap public lands, and refused to recognize the judgment of the Supreme Court regarding the rights of the Native American tribes.

For better or for worse, the Age of Jackson imbued the young nation with the raw ingredients it would need to reach its potential. The country believed in its power to do whatever it wanted to do; very different from the established, traditional model of nations long settled into their routines, America was evolving.

Jackson's imprint on the Democratic Party was a powerful one. His support of the common people over the interests of the moneyed and landed elite became a popular rallying cry for the new political group, but also branded a recurring theme in the American electorate.

Perhaps nothing so symbolically explains the transformation of the nation that Jackson governed better than the dilemma over the twenty-dollar bill which bears Jackson's image. The campaign to put a woman's image on American currency by 2020, in celebration of the centennial of women's suffrage, meant that one of the current images would be replaced. The original plan was to redesign the $10 bill, which bears the image of Alexander Hamilton - who, unlike Jackson, did like banks. But the success of a Broadway musical about the life of the Founding Father, who was, in his way, as controversial as Andrew Jackson, may have influenced the decision to target the $20 bill instead.

The campaign, which involved everyone from schoolchildren to former Federal Reserve Chairman Ben Bernanke voicing an opinion, captured the nation's imagination and sense of justice; in 2016, the Department of the Treasury made its decision. The front of the new $20 bill will bear the image of Harriet Tubman, the escaped slave who led other slaves to freedom along the Underground Railroad in the years before the Civil War. Andrew Jackson will be on the back of the bill, next to an image of the White House that he occupied as the People's President.

Some would say that Jackson is being demoted. Others say that his actions and views belonged to another era in American history, a time when women, slaves, and Native Americans were subject to the authority of all-powerful white men who gave little thought to the rights and freedoms of ethnic groups and the gender that were regarded as inferior.

But just as America is not the country it was when Jackson represented the potential of the common man, neither is the Jackson who governed in the 19 th century the only representation of America. Jackson was himself a bold experiment in power; he was born to poor parents who bestowed upon their only surviving son a drive to succeed, a love of freedom, and a determination to live according to his own creed. He was an American who loved his country and served his nation the best that he could.

Instead of seeing the change in the $20 bill as a reduction of Jackson's influence, perhaps it's more realistic to regard the inclusion of Harriet Tubman as a sign that America is always changing, always evolving, always expanding its boundaries, whether in territory as in the past or philosophy. Harriet Tubman and Andrew Jackson, together, represent America. Like Jackson, Harriet Tubman rose from the humblest of beginnings to achieve success and renown. Like Jackson, Tubman served in the military, in her case working as a nurse, scout, cook, and spy for the Union Army. Like the former general who used his gun to face down potential deserters who wanted to return home, Harriet Tubman, when a frightened slave wanted to turn back, pulled out a gun and kept her group intact. Like the former president, the former abolitionist showed courage in the face of danger.

Each one represents the face of America. The president who changed his country, and the presidency, remains a legend.

Made in the USA
Middletown, DE
29 January 2018